Stratford Library Association
2203 Main Street
Stratford, CT 06615
203-385-4160

W9-BZY-010

Genocide

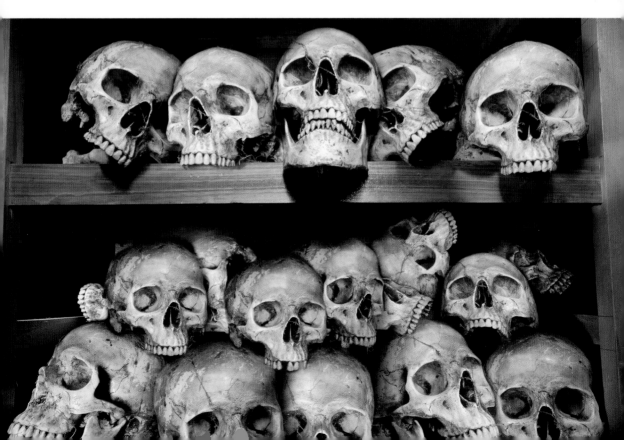

Critical World Issues

CRITICAL WORLD ISSUES

Genocide

Albert Ward

MASON CREST
PHILADELPHIA

Mason Crest
450 Parkway Drive, Suite D
Broomall, PA 19008
www.masoncrest.com

Printed and bound in the United States of America.

CPSIA Compliance Information: Batch #CWI2016.
For further information, contact Mason Crest at 1-866-MCP-Book.

First printing
1 3 5 7 9 8 6 4 2

Library of Congress Cataloging-in-Publication Data

on file at the Library of Congress
ISBN: 978-1-4222-3656-7 (hc)
ISBN: 978-1-4222-8136-9 (ebook)

Critical World Issues series ISBN: 978-1-4222-3645-1

Table of Contents

KEY ICONS TO LOOK FOR:

 Words to Understand: These words with their easy-to-understand definitions will increase the reader's understanding of the text, while building vocabulary skills.

 Sidebars: This boxed material within the main text allows readers to build knowledge, gain insights, explore possibilities, and broaden their perspectives by weaving together additional information to provide realistic and holistic perspectives.

 Research Projects: Readers are pointed toward areas of further inquiry connected to each chapter. Suggestions are provided for projects that encourage deeper research and analysis.

 Text-Dependent Questions: These questions send the reader back to the text for more careful attention to the evidence presented there.

Series Glossary of Key Terms: This back-of-the book glossary contains terminology used throughout this series. Words found here increase the reader's ability to read and comprehend higher-level books and articles in this field.

What Is Genocide?

For most of his adult life, Muhamed Cehajic worked as a teacher. He lived in a small city called Prijedor, which had a population of about 90,000. It was located in the province of Bosnia, which for most of the twentieth century was part of a country called Yugoslavia.

Yugoslavia had been created shortly after World War I ended in 1918, by uniting several provinces in southeastern Europe where Slavic peoples lived. However, by the late 1980s tensions were beginning to show among Yugoslavia's different ethnic and religious groups. One group, the Serbs, were led by a man named Slobodan Milosevic. He was president of the Serbian Republic, which like Bosnia was part of Yugoslavia. However, Milosevic wanted to expand his province and create a "Greater Serbia" that would be open to all of the ethnic Serbs from Yugoslavia.

United Nations forensic experts unearth victims from a mass grave in Bosnia. The victims were killed by Bosnian Serb soldiers in Srebrenica during July 1995.

At this time Prijedor was inhabited by two communities—Bosniaks, who were mainly Muslims, and Serbs, who were predominantly Orthodox Christians. These two groups of people had been enemies in the past, but for forty years they had lived peacefully side by side. Muhamed was a Muslim, but he knew and liked many Serbs.

In 1990, when he was 51, Muhamed decided to run for office as mayor of the city. The entire Muslim community

📖 Words to Understand in This Chapter

abduction—taking someone away by force.

anti-Semitism—prejudice against Jews.

atrocity—a shockingly cruel act, usually involving violence.

classification—the allocation of items or people into groups according to type.

concentration camp—a prison camp used in war for the incarceration of political prisoners or civilians.

dehumanization—the process of removing a person's or group's human qualities, in the eyes of others.

economic depression—a long period when trade is very slack, marked by high unemployment and poverty.

ghetto—a run-down area of a city lived in by a minority group, especially a group experiencing discrimination.

polarization—the process of exaggerating the differences between items or people so that those differences become ever more clear-cut s and extreme.

propaganda—organized publicity, often by a government, to promote a particular view.

refugee—someone who is seeking refuge, especially from war or persecution, by going to a foreign country.

symbolization—the process of identifying a particular group with a symbol.

A Bosnian Serb T-54 tank passes through the Bosnian village of Modrica in January 1995. Like most genocides, the ethnic cleansing inflicted by Serbs on Bosnian Muslims in the early 1990s required planning and organization.

voted for him, and he won the election. Muhamed was very happy in his new job, and worked hard for the city. Then, the following year, catastrophe struck. Civil war broke out in Yugoslavia, and the country began to fall apart.

The province of Bosnia declared its independence from Yugoslavia in 1992. Most of Bosnia's population was Muslim, although it had a large Serbian minority who wished to remain part of Yugoslavia. Milosevic ordered the national army of Yugoslavia, which was dominated by Serbs, to attack Sarajevo,

A Bosniak man mourns the loss of his wife and daughter at a cemetery in Sarajevo, 1993.

Bosnia's capital city. Serb snipers terrorized the city by shooting down civilians in the streets. There were many casualties, including 3,500 children.

The Bosnian Muslims were no match for the Yugoslav army, and the Serbs gradually took control of the region. As each town was captured, they rounded up the local Muslim population and either imprisoned them in *concentration camps* or, in some cases, massacred them. Women and girls were frequently the victims of rape. The plan was to turn Bosnia into a purely Serbian province. The process became known as "ethnic cleansing."

In the spring of 1992, Serb army forces took control of Prijedor. They ordered Muhamed to go on the radio and tell the people of the city to surrender their weapons to the Serbs. Instead, Muhamed told the citizens to remain calm and to use peaceful means to resist the illegal Serb government that the army had formed.

Prison Camp

Muhamed was removed from his job as mayor, and later arrested by Serb police. He was sent to a prison camp in a nearby city called Omarska. Prisoners at Omarska slept on the floor, and were fed one meal a day—a slice of bread and a bowl of thin soup. Conditions were filthy, and lice infested the prisoners' hair and beards. They were regularly tortured and beaten, and many did not survive.

Muhamed was held at Omarska for five weeks. Then, one night toward the end of July, 1992, he and six others—all high-ranking men from Prijedor—were led away by guards. They were never seen again. Muhamed was killed for no other reason than because he was a Muslim, and a leader of his community. Sadly, his story is not unusual.

The Western powers tried through diplomatic means to bring the fighting to an end. Safe havens were established by the UN, but these were ignored by the Serbs. In one safe haven, at Srebrenica, a Serbian force rounded up 7,500 Muslim men and boys between the ages of 12 and 60, and slaughtered them in July 1995.

The North Atlantic Treaty Organization (NATO), an international organization established in 1949 by the United States and countries of western Europe to promote international defense and collective security, responded to this *atrocity*. They launched a major bombing campaign, attacking Serb positions throughout Bosnia. The Serbs found they had no choice but to negotiate. A peace deal was agreed to in 1995. By this time, however, 200,000 Muslims had been massacred; over 20,000 were missing, feared dead; and two million Muslims had become *refugees*.

What Is Genocide

Genocide is defined as any action aimed at the destruction of a group of people, such as a nation, an ethnic group, or a race. An ethnic group is a community whose members shares a similar culture or background, and a race is a group of people who share similar physical characteristics, such as skin color and/or physical features.

The term "genocide" was invented in 1944 by a Polish-American legal expert named Raphael Lemkin. He decided a new word was needed to describe the large-scale, deliberate massacres that the Nazis were carrying out against the Jews and other ethnic or national groups at that time living in the parts of Europe that had been occupied by the armies of Nazi Germany. Lemkin combined the Greek word *genos*, meaning race or tribe, and *–cide* from the Latin word for killing.

Ever since the word genocide was created, there has been a debate about its exact meaning, and about what it should include. Some have argued that the term should include only actions that cause death. Others believe that the destruction of culture, religion, and language are also serious crimes worthy

Dr. Raphael Lemkin, who coined the word "genocide," also helped to draft the UN Genocide Convention in 1948. This international legislation was intended to prevent and punish the crime of genocide—the mass destruction of national, ethnic, racial, or religious groups.

of being called genocide. There are also arguments over what kinds of groups can be considered victims of genocide. As well as national, ethnic, and racial groups, some insist that political groups or economic classes can also suffer from a genocidal attack.

How Is Genocide Defined?

The United Nations (UN), an organization of countries formed after World War II, passed a law in 1948 making genocide illegal. The UN defined "genocide" as any act committed with intent to destroy in whole or in part a national, ethnic, racial, or religious group. This included the following kinds of activity:

- Killing members of the group.
- Causing serious bodily or mental harm to members of the group.

- Deliberately inflicting on the group conditions of life calculated to bring about its physical destruction in whole or in part.
- Imposing measures intended to prevent births within the group.
- Forcibly transferring children of the group to another group.

According to this definition, the attempt to destroy a political movement or economic class would not be classed as genocide. Cases like these may, however, be treated as "crimes against humanity." The UN also limited its definition to physical or psychological attacks, and did not include acts that attack a group's cultural or religious identity.

What Are the Six Stages of Genocide?

Genocide occurs for many different historical and political reasons, but different occurrences tend to have certain features in common. Researchers have attempted to identify these common features in the hope that this might increase the chances of predicting and preventing them in the future. Genocide expert Dr. Gregory Stanton has suggested that there are six stages in the build-up to genocide:

1. *Classification.* A government or group wishing to carry out genocide will first classify who is included in the group they wish to destroy. Classification can be done on the basis of physical appearance, for

The United Nations in session. Despite passing a law against genocide, the UN has often been unable to stop genocidal massacres taking place in the years since 1948.

example, or religion, or other characteristics.

2. *Symbolization.* The next stage is the development of symbols, which are used to identify the victim group and to mark them out physically. In Nazi Germany, for example, Jews were required to wear a yellow star on their clothing that identified them as Jewish and differentiated them from other citizens.

3. *Dehumanization.* In the third stage, the victim group is no longer thought of as human beings. Members of the group are likened to animals, ver-

min, or diseases, to make the idea of murdering them seem less abnormal.

4. Organization. Unlike a massacre, genocide is generally planned and organized. Special paramilitary units may be armed and trained to carry out the attacks.

5. *Polarization.* The victim group is physically separated from the rest of the population. Laws may forbid intermarriage or social interaction.

6. Preparation. The victim group is placed in camps, or forced into areas where they cannot grow food or sustain themselves. Death lists are drawn up. This stage occurs immediately before the genocide itself begins.

Blue Scarves

An example of the "symbolization" stage in the build-up to genocide occurred in Cambodia during 1975. The Cambodian government (known as the Khmer Rouge) had decided that the people living in the provinces of eastern Cambodia were enemies of the people and should be relocated and eliminated. To mark them out, they issued every man, woman, and child with a blue-and-white-checked scarf, known as a *kroma*. The Khmer Rouge insisted that Eastern Zone people wear these scarves at all times.

In Nazi Germany, Jews were required to wear a yellow Star of David on their clothing to identify themselves as Jewish, and thus second-class citizens—an example of symbolization.

Not all these stages have to happen. Some potential genocides may never progress beyond stages two or three. However, Stanton's analysis—and others like it—provides governments and international observers with a useful guide to help them monitor potential genocides around the world.

What Was the Holocaust?

The Holocaust was the attempt by Nazi Germany to wipe out the Jews of Europe. Around six million Jews were killed out of an estimated total population of eight million. There have been other genocides before and since, but the Holocaust remains a unique event in history. For the first time, the full power of a modern industrial state was used to transport, enslave, and slaughter an entire people.

The bodies of dead inmates fill the yard of Nordhausen, a Nazi concentration camp. This photo was taken shortly after the camp's liberation by the U.S. Army in 1945.

The Nazi Party, under Adolf Hitler's leadership, took power in Germany in 1933. They were fiercely *anti-Semitic* (prejudiced against Jews). They blamed the Jews for all of Germany's problems, such as defeat in World War I and *economic depression*. In fact, German Jews were very supportive of their country, and many had fought in the German army in World War I.

The Nazis introduced laws to separate the Jews from the rest of society, preventing them from marrying, socializing, or working with other Germans. *Propaganda* was used to persuade the population that Jews were dangerous and not to be trusted. World War II began in 1939 and the German occupation of Poland brought millions of Jews under Nazi control. Jews were separated from the rest of the population by being forced to live in rundown areas called *ghettos*.

In 1941, following the German invasion of the Soviet Union, the Nazis began massacring thousands of Jews and

Witness to a Massacre

During the Nazi invasion of the Soviet Union, execution squads followed the advancing German army, massacring the Jewish population of captured towns. An eyewitness recalls events in a small Ukrainian town in August 1941: "For about two hours, some three hundred men, including children aged fourteen, were seized in the streets or driven from their homes," reports the witness, as quoted in Martin Gilbert's book *Never Again: A History of the Holocaust*. "The Germans did not take part in the *abductions*. This was carried out with clear conscience by our Ukrainian neighbors who had lived side by side with the Jews for generations. . . . The job of shooting the victims was performed by the German murderers, whose superior training prepared them for it. At six o'clock in the evening, the whole thing was over."

The *Srebrenica-Potocari* memorial and cemetery for the victims of the 1995 genocide in Bosnia.

burying them in mass graves. That year, the Nazis secretly decided to exterminate all European Jews. Death camps were built in Poland, at Auschwitz, Chelmno, Belzec, Sobibor, Treblinka, and Majdanek. Millions of Jews were transported to these camps from all over occupied Europe. Most were killed with poisonous gas, and their bodies were then burned. The Holocaust was only stopped when the Nazis were defeated by the Allies in 1945.

 # Text-Dependent Questions

1. What is the definition of genocide?
2. According to Dr. Gregory Stanton, what are the six stages of genocide?

 # Research Project

Using the Internet or your school library, do some research on the definition of genocide, and answer the following question: "Should the Definition of Genocide be Widened to Include Other Kinds Of Mass Killing?" An argument in favor of this is that mass killing is equally bad, so its seriousness should not depend on whether the victims form a particular group. On the other hand, some people believe that if you widen the definition too far, the word genocide might lose its power. Write a two-page report with your conclusion and share it with your class.

Has There Always Been Genocide?

T hroughout history, peoples have been massacred, enslaved, or deported—either by their own leaders, or by outside conquerors. Genocides were generally planned in advance and carefully organized, but they also often occurred as a by-product of war and conquest. For example, in ancient times, it was common for captured cities or towns to be burned to the ground and their inhabitants massacred.

Between 1100 and 600 BCE, the Assyrians used what might be described as genocidal methods for maintaining control of their empire in the Middle East. They slaughtered thousands of prisoners of war as sacrifices to their supreme god. Those who rebelled against their rule were beheaded, impaled on stakes, or thrown alive into giant ovens. In 722 BCE, the Assyrians captured the kingdom of Northern Israel. Those Jewish residents

A depiction of warriors from the Ishtar Gate of ancient Babylon, built during the seventh century BCE. In the ancient world, victorious armies were generally ruthless in their treatment of conquered people.

who were not killed were deported to Mesopotamia (a region covering what is now Iraq, and parts of Turkey and Syria). The same thing occurred when the Babylonians conquered the kingdom of Judah (southern Israel) in 586 BCE.

Carthage was a powerful city-state on the coast of North Africa between the sixth and third centuries BCE. From 264 BCE, it became involved in a series of wars with the rival city-state of Rome. By 149 BCE, Carthage had lost all its colonies, and the Roman army had lain siege to the city itself. Carthage held out for three years before finally surrendering. The Romans stormed the city and began massacring its population. The killing lasted six days. By the time they were finished, only about 50,000 Carthaginians, out of an original population of 250,000, remained alive. They were sold into slavery. The Romans burned the city to the ground, ripped up its stones, and plowed over the land in their determination that Carthage would never rise again.

The persecution of minorities living within a larger community is another common event in history. Many Christians were killed under the Roman emperor Nero, who ruled from

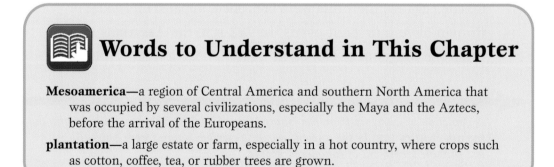

Words to Understand in This Chapter

Mesoamerica—a region of Central America and southern North America that was occupied by several civilizations, especially the Maya and the Aztecs, before the arrival of the Europeans.

plantation—a large estate or farm, especially in a hot country, where crops such as cotton, coffee, tea, or rubber trees are grown.

The Israelites, led by Joshua, cross the Jordan River as described in the Jewish and Christian scriptures. In the Book of Deuteronomy, God commands the Israelites to commit genocide as they are conquering the land of Canaan. "When the Lord your God brings you into the land you are entering . . . and you have defeated them, then you must destroy them totally. Make no treaty with them, and show them no mercy."

54 to 68 CE. According to a Roman historian, Nero covered them in the skins of wild animals and had them torn apart by dogs, or he used them as human torches to light the gardens of his palace. During the next 250 years, other Roman emperors also led persecutions of Christians until the religion was finally granted protection by the Emperor Constantine after 312 CE.

During the 1400s CE, the Aztecs of *Mesoamerica* sacrificed many thousands of war prisoners to their gods. In 1490, some 20,000 victims from an enemy tribe were massacred to cele-

This illustration shows the Egyptian Pharaoh Ramses II riding into battle against the Hittites in 1300 bce. The historical record shows that the Egyptians, like other ancient peoples, enslaved and mistreated the people that they conquered, such as the Nubians and the Hebrews.

brate the completion of a new pyramid. The line of doomed people was said to have stretched for almost two miles outside the Aztecs' capital city, Tenochtitlan. After it was over, the stench of rotting flesh hung over the city for weeks.

During the Middle Ages, the people of Christian Europe were often intolerant of minorities. Jewish communities were frequently the victims of massacres. During the 13th century the Roman Catholic Church established the Inquisition, the goal of which was to root out heresy. Thousands of Jews and Muslims who refused to give up their beliefs were tortured and put to death. In 1492, Muslims and Jews were expelled from Spain. In Russia and other places in eastern Europe, Jews were often the target of violent riots, called pogroms. The violence against Jews in Russia culminated with a series of pogroms from the 1880s through the 1910s, which led many Jews to emigrate to the United States.

Colonialism and Genocide

Beginning in the fifteenth century, European powers such as England, Spain, France, and Portugal began to colonize various parts of the world. Their arrival in the Americas, Africa, Asia, Australia, and the islands of the Pacific often brought disaster to the local populations. Although many natives died through mistreatment by their conquerors, by far the biggest killer was disease.

In 1519, Hernán Cortés led a small Spanish army that conquered the Aztec Empire of Mexico. The European conquerors regarded the natives they encountered as inferior beings, and saw nothing wrong with driving them off their lands and enslaving them.

For example, the native population of the Americas was devastated by exposure to influenza, typhoid, measles, and smallpox. They had no natural immunity to these diseases, and as a result, suffered losses of up to 80 or 90 percent of their original populations. The natives of the West Indies were virtually wiped out in just a few generations after the initial landing of Christopher Columbus in 1492.

American cavalry soldiers attack a Cheyenne village near the Sand Creek in Colorado, 1868. As the United States grew and expanded westward, Americans would often clash with the Native Americans they encountered.

Diseases also had a terrible impact on the natives of North American after the British arrived in places like Virginia and Massachusetts to establish colonies. As the colonies grew, they seized lands that the Indians had once roamed, often fighting wars against the tribes that had been living there for generations. After the United States gained independence, its government set into place a policy by which Native Americans were removed from their lands and compensated with other territories to the West. Eventually, these white settlers seized most of these lands as well, driving the natives out or attempting to exterminate them. In 1492, there had been around 8 million Native Americans living in the present-day United States. By 1890, when the government declared that the western frontier was closed, there were only 250,000 natives left.

The African Holocaust

The Europeans needed people to work on the *plantations* they established in their colonies, but because so many natives died, they were forced to look elsewhere for laborers. In the mid-1500s, Europeans began importing slaves from Africa to work in their American colonies. In the 1600s, two million slaves were transported from Africa to the Americas, and in the 1700s, the figure rose to six million. At the height of the slave trade, some parts of West Africa were almost emptied of people.

Slaves were mostly captured by their fellow Africans, who sold them to European traders. Once bought, the slaves were

The Tasmanian Aborigines

In the early 1800s, the Aboriginal people of Tasmania were virtually wiped out by European settlers. The Europeans took Aboriginal lands, enslaved their women, and killed many of their men. By 1835, only 135 out of an original population of about 4,000 remained alive. A minister named George Robinson took the survivors to a small island to be "Christianized." All but 47 of them died. The 4,000 Aborigines that live on Tasmania today are descendants of those 47 survivors.

A group of African men and boys being taken into slavery. Captives were force-marched from the African interior, escorted by armed slavers, to the coast, where they were loaded onto crowded and unsanitary ships that carried them across the Atlantic Ocean. Millions died during the journey.

branded like cattle and then herded onboard the ship. Conditions on the slave ships were appalling, and many died in the overcrowded, disease-ridden holds where they were held. It usually required between five and eight weeks to sail over the ocean. It is believed that between 10 and 40 percent of all the Africans taken across the Atlantic died during the arduous journey. Once in the New World (the Americas), slaves were sold once again, often at an auction. They then began their new life, usually as laborers on a plantation.

The African slave trade has been called a genocide because of the huge numbers of people deported, the dehumanizing way they were treated, and because so many died on the journey or soon after arrival. It has been called the "African Holocaust." It is believed that around 12 million Africans actually arrived in the Americas, and this figure does not include those who died on the journey. About 60 percent of the slaves went to Portuguese or Spanish colonies in Central America or South America. About 20 percent of the slaves went to British, French, or Dutch colonies in the Caribbean Sea. And about 20 percent of the slaves went to the British and French colonies on the mainland of North America (the present-day United States and Canada).

 **Text-Dependent Questions**

1. When did the Romans capture and destroy Carthage?
2. Why were the native populations of the Americas devastated by exposure to European diseases?
3. How many Native Americans were living in the United States in 1890?
4. How many Africans were brought across the Atlantic Ocean as slaves?

Research Project

Using the Internet or your school library, do some research on the definition of genocide, and answer the following question: "Did Europeans have the Right to take the Lands of the Native Populations in the Americas and Australasia?" On one hand, without the pioneering efforts of those original explorers and settlers, countries like the United States, Canada, and Australia would not exist today. However, the colonization of these lands caused the destruction of native cultures, some of them many thousands of years old. Write a two-page report, using data you've found in your research to support your conclusion.

What Are the Causes of Genocide?

I t is difficult for most people to imagine killing another human being, let alone taking part in a massacre. Yet genocides have occurred throughout history, and in many parts of the world. It is a mistake to believe that only certain peoples—usually in far-off lands—are capable of genocide. Under extreme enough circumstances, genocide could occur anywhere.

Genocides can sometimes happen in countries where two or more peoples with a history of grievances live closely together. The dominant group may seize the opportunity, during a war or some other national crisis, to right perceived historic wrongs done to their people. In Rwanda, where a genocide took place in the mid-1990s, the Hutu majority strongly resented the Tutsi people. This resentment dated from before 1962, when the Tutsi had been the dominant tribe.

← ──────────────────────────────

Human skulls fill a Buddhist stupa, or memorial, at the killing fields of Choeung Ek near Phnom Penh, Cambodia. The Khmer Rouge regime killed more than a million Cambodians between 1975 and 1979.

There was a similar underlying hostility between several of the ethnic groups in former Yugoslavia before civil war broke out in 1991. Serbs in the province of Kosovo claimed they were being mistreated by the Albanian Muslim majority. Serbs were also in the minority in Croatia, and many had died in massacres carried out by the pro-Nazi Croatian regime during World War II. The genocidal actions of the Serbs in the 1990s can partially be explained, but not justified, by pent-up hostility due to their treatment by other ethnic groups.

Genocides have often occurred as a result of conquest. A conquering army may use genocide as a tool of *repression*. For example, in 1937, the Japanese army marched into the Chinese city of Nanking and murdered half of the city's population of 600,000. Alternately, the leaders of an invading force may see genocide as the best means of bringing an occupied country, with a rebellious population, to submission.

An example of this occurred in Africa during the early twentieth century. Germany had established a *colony* in

Words to Understand in This Chapter

colony—a country or region ruled by another country.

communism—a system, or the belief in a system, in which capitalism is overthrown and control of wealth and property resides with the state.

deportation—the forcible removal of a person or people from a country.

rape—to force somebody to have sex.

repression—the exertion of strict control over the freedom of others.

segregate—to separate a person or group from the rest.

Japanese soldiers use bayonets to threaten Chinese captives, who are lying on the ground with their hands tied.

General Lothar von Trotha, commander of German forces in the Southwest Africa colony. In October 1904, von Trotha gave the following order: "Any Herero found within the German borders with or without a gun, with or without cattle, will be shot."

Hereroland, in southwest Africa, in 1885, but by 1903 the native Herero tribe had grown increasingly bitter about their treatment by the Germans. Large areas of their land had been taken away, making it impossible for the Hereros to continue their traditional way of life.

In 1904, the Hereros rose against the Germans, attacking farms, villages, and forts. Many of the colonists, including General Lothar von Trotha, the commander of the German forces, saw this uprising as an opportunity to wipe out the troublesome natives. The Hereros, armed with spears and wooden shields, were easily defeated by the Germans with modern rifles and artillery. Their only escape route was into the desert. The German military pursued the fleeing tribe. They prevented them from getting to sources of fresh water and killed men, women, and children indiscriminately. Many others died from starvation and thirst.

After two years, just 20,000 Hereros remained out of an original population of 80,000. With their leaders all killed, the remaining Hereros were reduced to a state of virtual slavery by the Germans, and all but ceased to exist as a tribe.

Prisoners in a Soviet labor camp work on a canal project near Belomorsk during the 1930s. Most of these men were imprisoned for being from the wrong political class, or because they were suspected of opposing the Soviet regime.

Most genocides are provoked by hatred of a racial or ethnic group arising out of conquest or historic grievances. However, over the past century some genocides have been motivated by a desire to create an ideal society. In these cases, the victims have been mainly political classes, who are seen as representing the "old society" that must be destroyed. This was the background to many of the mass killings, persecutions, and *deportations* that have occurred in *communist* countries, such as the Soviet Union under Josef Stalin, in the People's Republic of China under Mao Zedong and his successors, and in Cambodia under the Khmer Rouge during the 1970s.

Genocide in Bangladesh

For nine months in 1971, the Bengali people of East Pakistan fought a successful war of independence against Pakistan, to

Between 1958 and 1962, Chinese leader Chairman Mao Zedong's policies, known as the "Great Leap Forward," resulted in the deaths of an estimated 40 million Chinese peasants.

form the new nation of Bangladesh. In the course of this war, the Pakistani army committed a genocide that resulted in the deaths of approximately 1.5 million people.

The Bengali nationalists had won an election in 1970, but the Pakistani authorities prevented them from taking power. So, the nationalists launched a nonviolent protest. In March, 1971, the Pakistani government decided to try to terrify the Bengalis into submission.

They authorized the army to attack the Bengali capital of Dhaka. Thousands of unarmed civilians were killed in the city and surrounding countryside, and many homes and properties were destroyed.

The Pakistani forces targeted all able-bodied men, whether they were armed or not. During the campaign, they also abducted and *raped* approximately 200,000 girls and women. Ten million Bengalis were forced to take refuge in neighboring India. The killing finally ended in December when the Pakistanis were defeated by a combined Indian and Bengali army.

What Conditions are Needed for Genocide?

For a genocide to occur, a number of conditions must usually exist. Firstly, there is often an extreme threat of some kind, such as an economic collapse or a war. The economic depression suffered by Germany in the early 1930s, or the invasion that occurred in Rwanda in the 1990s, are examples of this. In such circumstances, people can revert to primitive behavior, believing they face a choice of "kill or be killed."

Secondly, a minority group needs to exist within this threatened society that can, however illogically, be blamed for the crisis. The German Jews, for example, were accused of a whole range of

"Since genocide takes planning, human rights violations must be seen as early warning signals of conflict and mass atrocities. When you see people at risk of atrocity crimes, do not wait for instructions from afar. Speak up, even if it may offend. Act. Our first duty must always be to protect people – to protect human beings in need and distress."

—UN Secretary-General Ban Ki-moon, at a July 2014 ceremony marking the 20th anniversary of the Rwandan genocide

Adolf Hitler making a speech in 1939. Hitler and the other Nazi leaders hated the Jews and, when they took power in Germany, they were able to turn their anti-Semitism into government policy.

sins in the 1920s and 30s, including growing rich on the miseries of others during the depression, plotting a communist revolution, and causing Germany's defeat in World War I. Some even believed there was a Jewish plot to take over the world. In Cambodia, where a genocide occurred during the 1970s, the city people were blamed by the peasants for keeping them in poverty by charging high interest on loans and paying low prices for their crops.

Thirdly, a genocide requires leadership. It cannot happen spontaneously. Someone needs to turn a general sense of anger and hatred into an organized policy of persecution and violence. Leaders like Adolf Hitler of Nazi Germany, Pol Pot of Cambodia, and Mao Zedong of China were very clever at expressing people's fears, stirring up their emotions, and intensifying their loathing toward a particular group. Such leaders were able to make the target group appear less than human, and therefore easier to kill. Leaders who inspire genocides often encourage their followers in the belief that they themselves are the victims. Whether their enemies are Jews, Muslims, or Tutsis, the message is usually the same—they are the ones who are persecuting us.

The degree to which leaders actually cause genocides varies from case to case, and is often a matter of debate. Some historians continue to argue over the degree of Hitler's involvement in the decision to exterminate the Jews. He issued no written order, and it is uncertain whether he even gave a verbal command to enact the "final solution," which we call the Holocaust. Yet it was Hitler and his extreme anti-Semitism that was the major driving force behind the Nazi persecution of the

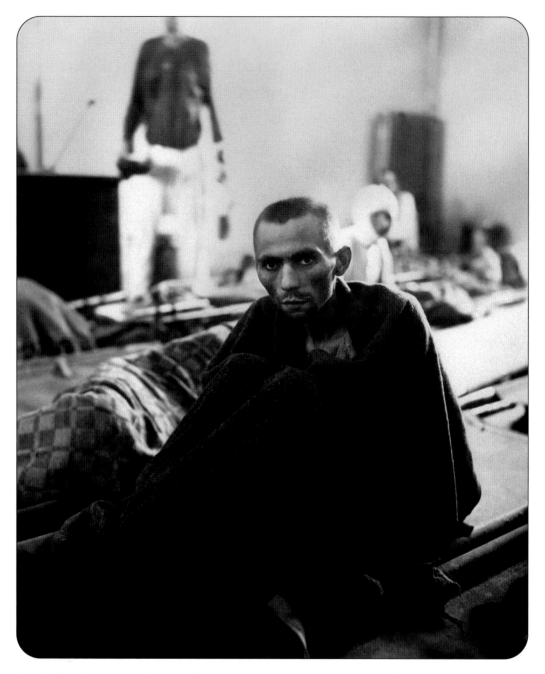

A starving inmate at the Mauthausen-Gusen concentration camp, the largest Nazi concentration camp in Austria during World War II.

Jews. Without him, it is difficult to imagine the Holocaust occurring.

A fourth condition required for a genocide to occur is organization. A leader acting alone cannot bring about a genocide, He needs loyal followers to carry out his wishes. People need to be armed and trained; victims need to be identified and *segregated*; methods of killing and disposal of bodies need to be established. All this requires planning and resources, which is why genocides are almost always carried out by governments. Usually only those in power have the ability to organize the systematic slaughter of large groups of people.

Text-Dependent Questions

1. What tribal group did the Hutu people in Rwanda strongly resent? Why?
2. How did German colonial leaders attempt to exterminate the Herero people?
3. What belief do the leaders that inspire genocides often encourage in their followers?

Research Project

Using the Internet or your school library, do some research on the definition of genocide, and answer the following question: "Under certain conditions, such as those discussed in this chapter, do you think anyone is capable of taking part in a genocide?" Some will contend that people are all essentially the same, and under extreme enough circumstances, any one could kill. Others believe that if people are taught to respect other cultures, and to appreciate our common humanity, there is no reason why a genocide should ever occur. Write a two-page report, using data you've found in your research to support your conclusion, and present it to your class.

Infamous Genocides

O ver the past century, numerous incidents of mass killings have taken place. Although they occurred at different times and in different places, similar patterns emerge: ruthless leaders, the willingness of their subordinates to carry out brutal orders, and the helplessness of victims.

The Armenian Genocide

In 1914, the Muslim Ottoman Empire was in deep decline. The Ottoman Empire was a Turkish empire that had been established during the late 1200s in Asia Minor. At the empire's height, during the sixteenth and seventeenth centuries, the Ottoman sultans ruled a vast area of the Middle East, eastern Europe, and north Africa. However, by the early twentieth cen-

This ceremony in Istanbul was held to remember the murder of Armenians conducted within the Ottoman Empire in the early twentieth century. Controversially, the Turkish government refuses to classify atrocities committed against Armenians between 1915 and 1923 as genocide.

tury the Ottomans' power was severely weakened, and the empire was ruled by a dictatorial regime known as the Young Turks. The Armenians, a Christian people living in an eastern region of the empire, wished for independence. They turned for support to France and Britain.

The Young Turks suspected these countries of wishing to take over parts of its empire, and they feared an alliance between the Armenians and the European powers. The solution to their problem, the Young Turks decided, would be to eliminate the Armenians altogether. They found an opportunity, while Europe was preoccupied with World War I, to put their plan into action.

Beginning in April 1915, young, male Armenians were disarmed, placed in labor camps, and either worked to death or executed. Leading members of the Armenian community—among them doctors, lawyers, academics, and ministers—were arrested and taken away, never to be seen again.

 Words to Understand in This Chapter

decapitate—to cut off someone's head.

guerrilla—a member of an unofficial military force, usually with some political aim such as the overthrow of a government.

Islam—the religion of Muslims, based on the teachings of the seventh-century prophet Mohammed.

machete—a large, heavy, broad-bladed knife used as a tool for cutting through vegetation, or as a weapon.

unsanitary—not clean.

The dead bodies of Armenians, mostly men with a few women, are displayed outside a building. This photograph was received by the American Red Cross in February 1919 as evidence of the genocide.

An Armenian Girl's Story

Takouhi Levonian was fifteen at the time of the deportations. She and her family were forced to leave their home town of Keghi in May 1915. After six days, they reached the town of Palu. There, Taki's father was taken away by the Turkish police. She never saw him again. The next day, her group was attacked by Turks and Kurds. Some were shot. Her aunt's husband was beaten in the head with an ax and his body was dumped in the river. They walked on for fifteen days. There was little food and water. Their shoes had worn away, and Taki wrapped cloth around her bare feet to ease the pain. For three full days, they went without water, and one of her siblings died. Eventually, Takouhi, her mother, and her sister arrived at a camp for refugees where they were safe.

Meanwhile, the rest of the population—mostly women, children, and the elderly—were driven from their homes, and herded toward the Syrian desert. Some traveled by wagon or train, but most went on foot carrying only the barest essentials.

The intention of the deportations was to drive the Armenians out into remote, unprotected areas where they could be destroyed. Many were robbed of their possessions, and children were kidnapped. Others died of starvation, or were attacked by killing units who slaughtered them with swords, regardless of age or gender.

Only a quarter of the population survived the terrible journey. Many of those later died in the blistering heat of the desert. Others were butchered by killing units at a place called Deir el-Zor. In all, around one million Armenians died in the genocide of 1915–1916.

Today, most scholars of genocide, as well as the leaders of dozens of countries, recognize the atrocities that were committed against Armenians in the Ottoman Empire as a genocide. However, the government of Turkey has maintained a controversial official position that the killings were merely an unfortunate consequence of the World War that was raging at the time, and not truly a genocide.

The Soviet Deportations

After the Nazi attack on the Soviet Union in 1941, the Soviet leader Josef Stalin was concerned that some of the nationalities living within the Soviet Union might side with the German invaders. Between late 1941 and the middle of 1944, eight ethnic groups were deported from the Soviet Union: the Germans, Balkars, Chechens, Crimean Tatars, Ingushi, Karachai, Kalmyks, and Meskhetians. In all, more than five million people were

Under Josef Stalin, Soviet officials removed more than five million people from their homes, resettling them in sparsely populated territories of the Soviet Union. It is estimated that about 1.5 million of these people died as a result of Stalin's resettlement policies.

forced from their homes.

The deportations were carried out with brutal efficiency. Military units appeared in towns and villages announcing a "transfer." The population was given only a very brief time to gather up a few belongings before being put on trains. No exceptions were made—not even for families of those serving in the armed forces or Communist Party members. They traveled in crowded, *unsanitary* conditions for hundreds of miles to remote regions in Kazakhstan, Siberia, and Central Asia. They were forced to work in mines, factories, and on farms.

Many died on the way, or soon after arrival, from hunger, cold, and disease. The Crimean Tatars lost 46 percent of their numbers in the first year and a half. About two-fifths of the Buddhist Kalmyks died by the end of the first year. Their original homes were looted and seized. Soviet authorities then changed place names, banned their languages, and rewrote the history books to make it seem as though these peoples had never existed.

The Rape of Nanking

The Japanese army invaded China in 1937. In December of that year, after a four-day battle, they captured the ancient Chinese city of Nanking (Nanjing). For the Japanese military leaders, their first concern was to remove any threat from the 90,000 Chinese soldiers who had surrendered. The Japanese had been trained to believe that surrendering was a contemptible act of cowardice, so they viewed the Chinese soldiers as unworthy of life. The soldiers were driven in trucks to remote locations near the city, where they were killed in the most cruel and sadistic ways. Some were used for bayonet practice. Others were *decapitated*. Some were soaked in gasoline and then set on fire.

The women of Nanking were the next Japanese target. More than 20,000 females, including elderly and pregnant women and young girls, were gang-raped by Japanese soldiers, then stabbed to death or shot. Throughout the city, soldiers fired their rifles into crowds of civilians, and set fire to buildings after locking people inside. Many residents of Nanking

Japanese soldiers celebrate the capture of Nanking in December 1937. They would soon go on a rampage of rape and murder in the city.

The Killing Contest

When Tang Shunsan, a Chinese resident of Nanking, was captured by the Japanese, he and a group of other prisoners were ordered to stand, several rows deep, in front of a freshly dug pit. The Japanese decided to have a contest to see who could kill their enemies the fastest. The soldiers split up into four teams of two, and began to behead the prisoners with their swords. The Chinese prisoners stood frozen with horror as their countrymen were slaughtered one by one. As the prisoner directly in front of Tang was decapitated, his body toppled backward against Tang, who was able to fall with it into the pit. Nobody noticed, and soon Tang was buried beneath headless bodies. Later, when the Japanese left the scene, Tang crawled out of the pit and escaped. He was the only one to survive this "killing contest."

were taken outside the city and forced to dig their own graves before being decapitated. Others were simply buried alive. The massacres continued for six weeks, until the beginning of February 1938. Corpses could be seen everywhere. It is said that the streets ran red with blood.

A brave group of American and European doctors and missionaries who were stationed in Nanking managed to set up an international safety zone in the middle of the city. They frequently risked their lives by intervening to prevent executions or rapes. About half the city's population of 600,000 took refuge in the safety zone. Almost all the others eventually perished.

Massacres in Indonesia

During the mid-1960s, the Indonesian Communist Party (PKI) looked to be on the verge of achieving power in this populous island nation. It had a vast membership numbering millions, and exercised growing influence within the Indonesian government. The PKI also had some powerful enemies: the Indonesian army was hostile to the PKI, because the party had its own military units, which were seen as a threat to the army's position. The *Islamic* community also feared a communist takeover. Indonesia was predominantly Muslim, but other communist regimes had banned the practice of religion and Islamic leaders feared the PKI would do the same if they gained power.

During 1965, some extremists made an attempt to seize power in Indonesia. Some members of the PKI may have been involved, although today this is not certain. At the time, however, most Indonesians believed that the communists were behind the attempted coup.

The anticommunist alliance of Muslims and the army took the opportunity to attack the PKI. Local Muslim leaders organized their followers into squads, and drew up lists of intended targets associated with the communists. The army helped by providing weapons and training. In some areas, the army itself carried out the attacks.

The massacres took place mostly at night. Victims were dragged from their beds and taken to remote places outside their villages. They were killed with bayonets or parangs, which are single-bladed *machetes* used by Indonesian peasants. The bodies were dumped in rivers or buried in shallow graves.

A few of the estimated 20,000 Cambodian men, women, and children suspected of being enemies of the revolution who were imprisoned by the Khmer Rouge in a secret detention center in Phnom Penh. They were tortured, forced to write false confessions, and then executed. Today, these portraits are on display at the Tuol Sleng Genocide Museum in Phnom Penh.

In most cases, the death squads killed only those named on their lists but, sometimes, entire villages associated with the PKI were slaughtered.

Approximately half a million people were killed in the massacres. As a result, the PKI was completely destroyed as a political force.

The Killing Fields of Cambodia

In 1975, a communist guerrilla force known as the Khmer Rouge took power in Cambodia. Its leader, Pol Pot, planned a radical experiment to completely transform the country into a communist peasant farming society. He declared that Cambodia had to be purified of all foreign influences, including urban life, business, and religion.

In the months that followed, Cambodia was gradually sealed off from the outside world. Foreigners were expelled, embassies were closed, and foreign languages were banned. Newspapers and television stations were shut down, and mail and telephone usage was restricted. Money was prohibited, businesses closed down, and religion, education, and public healthcare were all eliminated.

Cambodia's cities were then emptied of their inhabitants. They were forced from their homes and driven at gunpoint into the country. Two million were evacuated on foot from the capital city Phnom Penh, and as many as 20,000 died on the way. The former city-dwellers, unused to farm work, were forced to labor in the fields. They worked 18-hour days under the brutal supervision of armed soldiers, and were fed just one can of rice every two days. Many thousands died of overwork, malnutrition, and disease. The farms became known as the killing fields.

Throughout the country, purges were carried out to destroy the educated elite of the "old society." Tens of thousands of doctors, lawyers, teachers, academics, Buddhist monks, and officials of the old regime were all killed along with their families. The Khmer Rouge also attacked ethnic groups, including

Cambodians of Vietnamese or Chinese descent, as well as Cham Muslims. Anyone suspected of being disloyal to Pol Pot was shot. This included many of the former Khmer Rouge leaders! Up to 20,000 of Pol Pot's former supporters were tortured into giving false confessions of disloyalty before being executed.

The Khmer Rouge was overthrown in 1979 following a Vietnamese invasion of Cambodia. Its four years in power had resulted in the deaths of approximately two million people—a quarter of Cambodia's population.

The bodies of Rwandans who died during the genocide lie in the street, July 1994.

Young Rwandan children at a refugee camp in neighboring Zaire (Democratic Republic of the Congo). Many of these children witnessed the murders of their parents during the genocide.

Genocide in Rwanda

Rwanda is a small country in central Africa. It is home to two main ethnic groups: the Hutus and the Tutsis. The Hutus form around 90 percent of the population. Yet the Tutsis regard themselves as the elite, and during the period when Rwanda was a Belgian colony (1916 to 1962) the Tutsis had been the dominant tribe.

Following independence from Belgium, the majority Hutu seized power in Rwanda and reversed the roles of the two tribes. Their persecution of Tutsis caused 200,000 to flee to neighboring countries. These refugee Tutsis formed a *guerrilla* army which, in 1990, invaded Rwanda. They forced the president to sign an agreement to allow the Tutsis to share power with the Hutus.

In April 1994, following the assassination of Rwanda's Hutu president, Hutu extremists who had violently opposed the power-sharing plan went on a rampage. They murdered Tutsi leaders and moderate Hutu politicians. The violence spread into the country. Hutu military units, armed with machetes, clubs, guns, and grenades, roamed around slaughtering Tutsi civilians. All Rwandans carried identification cards specifying their tribe, and these cards were now being used to determine whether a person should live or die.

A Hutu Remembers

Joseph Rukwavu, a Hutu, was 74 when the massacres took place in Rwanda. "Two hundred were killed in my sector, even my wife, because she would not join Interahamwe [a Hutu force responsible for the massacres]," he told reporter Mark Fritz of the Associated Press in May 1994. "The militia gathered everybody up near a big hole. . . . [The Tutsi victims] were weeping, even the men. Even the week before we killed them they were weeping in fear. They said, 'Oh, we are the same people, we are your neighbors. Instead of hiding us you are killing us.'"

After ten Belgian soldiers serving with a UN peacekeeping force in Rwanda were tortured and murdered by Hutus, Western countries began evacuating their own citizens from Rwanda. Most of the UN peacekeeping force was also withdrawn. However, no effort was made to evacuate Tutsi civilians, who were left without any protection from the murderous Hutu militias.

In an attempt to escape the killing, some Tutsis hid in churches, but even these provided no refuge. In one church in Musha, 1,200 Tutsis were killed in a massacre that lasted all day. Even the wounded, who managed to get to a hospital, were often sought out and murdered in their beds. Some Hutus were forced by angry mobs to kill their Tutsi neighbors, and even members of their own families, to save their own lives.

The killings were only halted in July 1994 when Tutsis invaded from neighboring countries and defeated the Hutus. By then, around 800,000 people had been killed.

Massacres in Darfur

The region known as Sudan, in northeastern Africa, has been plagued by civil war since the mid-1950s. The northern part of Sudan is predominantly Muslim in religion and Arab in ethnicity. Southern Sudan is home to black African tribes who practice either Christianity or traditional African animist religions. The two regions waged a civil war from 1955 until 1972 that led to more than 500,000 deaths. The conflict resumed in 1983 and lasted until 2003, when a cease-fire was signed after more than a million more Sudanese deaths.

The North-South fighting subsided after the peace agree-

An Indonesian member of a peacekeeping force patrols a refugee camp in the Darfur region of western Sudan.

ment was implemented, but a new conflict soon emerged in a region of western Sudan known as Darfur. Unlike the North-South conflict, which was based on religious differences, the causes of the Darfur conflict were based more on ethnicity, politics, and economics. The two sides fighting in Darfur were both predominantly Muslim, although one group was of African ethnicity and the other is of Arab descent.

The Darfur conflict began as a rivalry between farmers and herdsmen over pastureland. The farmers, many of whom were of African descent, attempted to prevent nomadic herdsmen of Arab ethnicity, known as the Baggara, from grazing their flocks on land used for their crops. The Baggara responded by attacking villages and forcing out the farmers.

In 2003 two groups, the Justice and Equality Movement (JEM) and the Sudanese Liberation Army, rebelled against Sudan's government, claiming that it had sided with the Baggara by assisting an Arab militia called the janjaweed. Both sides were accused of significant human rights violations, including looting, rapes, mass killings, and the destruction of entire villages. In particular, the janjaweed was accused of carrying out a policy of "ethnic cleansing" in the Darfur region.

The African Union brokered a ceasefire in April 2004 and sent peacekeeping troops in to ensure compliance. However, the conflict continued, and by 2006 the United Nations estimated that over 400,000 people had been killed in Darfur, with another 2 million people driven from their homes. That year the UN proposed sending a larger peacekeeping force of more than 17,000 soldiers to replace the smaller African Union force. However, Sudan refused to allow the UN peacekeepers into the country. Instead, the government launched a major military offensive against the rebel groups.

Unlike Sudan's first and second civil wars, religion does not play an important part in the fighting, as most of the combatants on all sides are Muslims. Additionally, in recent years some groups of Darfuri Arabs have begun waging their own armed rebellion against the Arab government and its jan-

Former Bosnian Serb leader Radovan attends a church service with his wife Ljiljana Zelen in 1993. In March 2016, Karadzic was convicted of genocide, war crimes, and crimes against humanity by a United Nations tribunal. The 70-year-old was sentenced to forty years in prison for his role in ethnic cleansing operations in Bosnia, including the slaughter of nearly 8,000 Muslim men and boys in Srebrenica in 1995.

jaweed allies, which they say do not represent them.

During the years of fighting, there have been several cease-fire agreements in hopes of negotiating a peace. The most recent came in February 2010, when the Justice and Equality Movement agreed to talks with the Sudanese government. However, the talks have gone nowhere and sporadic violence by both sides has continued in the region.

 **Text-Dependent Questions**

1. Why were eight ethnic groups deported from the Soviet Union between 1941 and 1944?
2. Why were Indonesian Muslim leaders opposed to the communist PKI?
3. How many Cambodians were killed while the Khmer Rouge ruled the country in the 1970s?
4. In what country is the Darfur region located?

Research Project

Using the Internet or your school library, do some research on the definition of genocide, and answer the following question: "Is Genocide ever Inevitable (Sure to Happen)?" On one hand, some will say that if certain conditions arise, such as a hated minority, and an economic depression, genocide is almost certain to follow. Others believe that genocides happen because of the actions of ruthless leaders, and that social and economic factors cannot by themselves cause genocides to occur. Write a two-page report, using data you've found in your research to support your conclusion.

LEST THEY PERISH

CAMPAIGN *for* $30,000,000

AMERICAN COMMITTEE
FOR RELIEF IN THE NEAR EAST

ARMENIA - GREECE - SYRIA - PERSIA

ONE MADISON AVE., NEW YORK.   CLEVELAND H. DODGE, TREASURER

How Does Genocide Affect People?

Genocides can affect individual victims as well as whole communities for years, even decades, after the killing has stopped. Survivors must cope with the loss of loved ones, and are often plagued by painful memories. They have to try to rebuild their devastated lives, and deal with the practical issues of finding accommodation and food.

Genocide survivors who lack the means to take care of themselves or their families become refugees, dependent on the charitable activities of aid organizations. Some may be faced with injury or disfigurement as a result of wounds. The psychological scarring often never goes away, especially for child victims, and women who are raped during genocidal attacks.

Studies of Holocaust survivors have shown that virtually all suffered, to different degrees, from a condition known as "sur-

This 1917 poster is attempting to raise money to help Armenians in the Ottoman Empire. The American Committee for Relief in the Near East was formed in response to the genocide. It raised millions to help starving Armenians, and provided shelter and health care to survivors of the attacks.

vivor syndrome." Symptoms included severe anxiety, losses of memory and understanding, depression, and frequent illness. Most learned to live with their *trauma*, and managed to rebuild their lives, but others never recovered.

Many Cambodians remain, to this day, traumatized by the events of 1975–1979. The stress caused by their memories of the genocide has sometimes led to physical illnesses, including blindness.

Genocides can also destroy whole communities. Following the genocide of the Hereros in 1904, the Germans took steps to ensure the tribe would never rise again. By making it illegal for them to own land or cattle, restricting their movements, and dispersing them across hundreds of different farms, the Hereros were given no opportunity to return to their traditional lifestyle or reorganize as a tribe. Most became laborers for German farmers, with no separate identity of their own.

The Armenians also lost their homeland, and very nearly their identity, as a result of the 1915 genocide. So many were killed that whole towns and villages disappeared from the map.

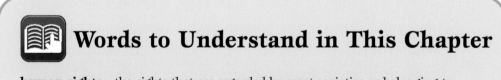 **Words to Understand in This Chapter**

human rights—the rights that are regarded by most societies as belonging to everyone, such as the rights to freedom, justice, and equality.

humanitarian—committed to improving the lives of other people.

stereotype—a standard, oversimplified image, often one that is negative.

trauma—an extremely distressing experience that can cause lasting psychological damage.

For survivors, the forced removal from their homes meant the loss of everything they owned, leaving them penniless.

The Armenians only survived as a people thanks to *humanitarian* aid from the United States. They were resettled in the Middle East, Russia, and North America. However, the Armenians' historic bond with their homeland was lost forever.

The Ukrainian nation suffered in a similar way in 1932–1933. Stalin ordered the seizure of all their farm produce because they had failed to meet food production targets. The famine that followed caused the deaths of between five and seven million people. The Ukrainian nation was crushed by this experience, their leadership was destroyed, and their language and culture clung on only in the rural areas.

This monument in Halabja, a town in the Kurdish region of Iraq, lists the names of approximately 5,000 people killed when Iraqi dictator Saddam Hussein launched a poison gas attack against the town. The attack was part of Saddam's al-Anfal campaign (1986–1988), in which he attempted to exterminate Kurdish citizens who did not support his government.

The Holocaust destroyed the once-thriving Jewish communities of eastern Europe. Hundreds of thousands of Jews, fearing anti-Semitism, decided not to return to their original homes after being liberated from the camps. Instead, many ended up going to the United States,

Tatars in traditional costume. The loss of their homeland through mass deportation during the Soviet era meant the loss of institutions, such as schools, libraries, newspapers, museums, and universities that were the storehouses of Tatar culture. This threatened the Tatars' very identity as a people.

Britain, and Palestine.

Some victim communities can react to genocides by becoming more violent themselves, as happened to Bangladeshi society after the 1971 genocide. This peaceful community had traditionally resolved conflicts through negotiation and compromise. However, nine months of mass killing, rape, and destruction had a brutalizing effect on the Bengali people. Students and young people became used to carrying arms and using violence to resolve disputes and settle scores. University campuses became the most dangerous places in the country.

A genocide inflicted by the Tutsis on the Hutus in Burundi in 1972, killing about 150,000 people, had a similar effect. The Hutus felt a violent anger toward the Tutsis, and a burning desire for revenge. This found its outlet in the 1994 genocide in Rwanda.

The Media and Genocide

The media has a crucial role to play in alerting the world to a genocide. Photographs and television news reports can show in graphic terms what is happening. In Bosnia, a famous photo of a starving prisoner in a Serbian prison camp helped to focus the world's attention on the unfolding tragedy in that country. In 2015, a shocking photograph of a three-year-old Syrian boy who drowned while trying to reach Europe with his family made international news. The photo drew attention to the crisis in Syria, where a civil war that began in 2011 had resulted in more than 300,000 deaths, displaced more than half of the country's population from their homes, and drove more than 4 million people to flee the country as refugees. While not technically a genocide by the UN definition, the situation in Syria has been characterized by numerous massacres and *human rights* violations.

Unfortunately, the world's media have often been slow to report genocides. By the time the journalists and cameras arrive on the scene, hundreds of thousands of people may already be dead. This is mainly because the governments responsible for genocides take steps to keep their actions a secret, and journalists are often banned from the scene.

When the world's media do get to report a genocide, its

A British Army officer serving with the UN peacekeeping operation in Bosnia speaks to the international media during a briefing in Sarajevo, September 1993.

efforts to publicize the story, however well-intentioned, do not always have positive effects. Journalists don't always have an in-depth understanding of the background to a genocide, and this can lead to a distorted view of the situation. For example, early in the Bosnian conflict, most foreign journalists portrayed it as simply a flaring-up of age-old ethnic tensions. They did not mention Serbian aggression.

Many modern newspapers and TV stations look upon news stories partially as opportunities to increase their share of the audience or readership. Journalists are therefore encouraged to focus on the sensational aspects of a genocide—including images of starving or wounded victims—with less emphasis on informing people about the root causes.

This focus on the immediate crisis pressurizes governments and international agencies to respond with short-term solutions, such as helping victims with money, medical aid, and shelter. This aid is necessary and helpful, but rebuilding a society following a genocide can take decades, and requires long-term solutions. Unfortunately, the media has a short attention span and, often within a few weeks, the world's cameras and

Television reporters interview a Syrian man in a refugee camp in Turkey near the border between the two countries. Often, "human interest" stories tend to dominate media coverage of genocides. As a result, the viewer is often left feeling sympathetic but uninformed about the causes of suffering.

microphones are pointing in a different direction, in another part of the world.

In some cases, it can be argued that the media can actually prepare a population for participation in a genocide. Newspapers in particular have been known to exploit the anxieties of certain sections of the public about the presence of a minority. In countries like the United States, Great Britain, and

Marching protesters call for UN intervention in Darfur. Such rallies can attract media attention and raise awareness of genocides.

Genocide of the Gypsies

As well as attempting to exterminate the European Jews, the Nazis also killed between a quarter and a half a million Roma and Sinti gypsies. A survivor of these purges, Leopoldine Papai, gave this account that was reprinted in the book *Century of Genocide: Eyewitness Accounts and Critical Views*:

> "My parents were killed in Auschwitz, my father died of typhus. . . . Shortly thereafter, my sister and I—together with many Jews—were sent to Ravensbruck. Many on this transport were shot, many died. After eight months, we were again deported . . . to Bergen-Belsen. That was the worst. There was absolutely nothing to eat there and we slept on the bare ground. The British freed us in Bergen-Belsen. There are only two of us alive out of 36 family members; my sister and I. . . . I have lung problems because of the camps and will probably never be completely healthy."

Syrian refugees arrive at a camp on the border with Turkey. In March 2016, US Secretary of State John Kerry declared that one of the factions in the Syrian civil war, the Islamic State of Iraq and the Levant (ISIL), was carrying out genocide against Christians and other minorities in Syria.

France, newspapers have published negative reports about asylum seekers (people seeking refuge from persecution), claiming that many of them are illegal immigrants in search of a more comfortable life, and that they go there simply to claim benefits, to steal, or to beg. These reports serve to reinforce a *stereotype* of asylum seekers in the public mind, and can be seen as the start of a process toward dehumanization.

 ## Text-Dependent Questions

1. What is "survivor syndrome"?
2. In what places were Armenian survivors of the genocide resettled?
3. Why is the world's media sometimes slow to report genocide?

Research Project

Using the Internet or your school library, do some research on the definition of genocide, and answer the following question: "Does the mass deportation of a people from their homeland amount to a Genocide?" Some scholars will note that a people's identity is strongly wrapped up with where they live, and the loss of a homeland can mean the death of a culture. Others contend that a people can survive the loss of a homeland, and that mass deportation cannot be compared to an attempt to exterminate them. Write a two-page report, using data you've found in your research to support your conclusion, and present it to your class.

Can Genocide Be Stopped?

T he institutions that had been established to try to prevent genocide—most notably the United Nations—have, so far, not succeeded in doing so. Many minorities around the world are still at risk of genocide. Effective methods of preventing genocides from happening in the future need to be developed urgently.

Much research has gone into the development of an effective "early warning system" for genocide. The aim of such a system would be, firstly, to predict future genocides by looking out for the telltale signs, such as dehumanizing propaganda or the isolation of minorities. A network of organizations in a permanent state of readiness would be employed for this task.

Once a genocide has been predicted, the next task would be to investigate the allegations, probably by a UN office set up for

Refugees from East Timor prepare to board a ship that will return them to their homes in Dili. Many people were driven away in a campaign of terror waged by the Indonesian military in 1999.

this purpose. If the allegation proves genuine, the media would be alerted to the developing crisis. Pressure would be applied on governments and international bodies to intervene and prevent the genocide from taking place.

Such a system sounds very good in theory, but it has proved difficult to establish for several reasons. First, genocides often take place during wars or revolutions, when the situation is chaotic and difficult for outsiders to observe or understand. Reports from refugees and eyewitnesses are not always reliable, and by the time *objective* international observers are in place many thousands might already be dead. Sometimes, as in Indonesia in 1965, a genocide seems to start suddenly, with no clear warning. Therefore, one of the biggest challenges in trying to stop genocides is learning how to predict them.

Once a genocide has been identified and the alert has been sounded, the next task is coaxing the international community to respond. Various levels of response are possible, usually beginning with an official protest against the guilty state. This is rarely effective, but at least serves warning that genocidal actions have been observed.

Words to Understand in This Chapter

impending—about to happen.

objective—free of any prejudice caused by personal feelings.

sanctions—measures taken by other countries to place economic pressure on a government, in order to force leaders to change their course of action.

The Dallaire Fax

The need for a genocide "early warning system" was highlighted during the Rwandan genocide of 1994. In January of that year, the commander of the UN peacekeeping force in Rwanda, General Romeo Dallaire, sent a fax to UN headquarters warning that genocide was being planned. His fax received a routine response, and no further action was taken. Other reports around this time, from diplomats and international organizations, also warned that ethnic tensions were rising in Rwanda. Despite these warnings, the UN and the world were taken by surprise when, only months later, the massacres began.

Victims or Perpetrators

Following a NATO campaign to end the Serb genocide against Albanian Muslims in Kosovo, reports began to surface of atrocities being carried out against Serbs by the Kosovo Liberation Army (KLA), an Albanian guerrilla group. This illustrates one of the risks of military intervention: action taken against perpetrators can encourage the victim group to retaliate with human rights violations of its own.

The next level of intervention is the use of *sanctions*—for example, by stopping trade with that country. Sanctions are

The UN Security Council discusses sanctions against those impeding peace in Sudan.

usually slow to take effect, and can sometimes harden attitudes within the targeted government. They can also make life even harder for the threatened minority.

If sanctions fail to have an impact, an international peacekeeping force may be sent in to try to stop massacres by separating the aggressors from their victims, establishing safety zones, and protecting food supplies. Problems arise because peacekeeping forces are not authorized to fight except in selfdefense. They are, therefore, sometimes unable to prevent atrocities from happening in front of them. This occurred, for example, in Srebrenica in Bosnia in 1995. Dutch peacekeeping troops surrendered 30,000 Muslim refugees to a Serbian force without resistance. A massacre of 7,500 men and boys followed.

The most extreme form of intervention is military action. This is often the only effective way of bringing a halt to a genocide. However, the risks are great. There are likely to be deaths among the soldiers sent to intervene. Such operations are very expensive, and may lead to long-term involvement in the affected country. Establishing clear-cut military goals at the outset is therefore essential.

Nepalese members of the UN peacekeeping force in Darfur stand at attention. Peacekeeping forces composed of international troops can play an important role in preventing new conflicts from emerging.

There is also the problem that in a conflict between ethnic groups, the issues are rarely black and white. In former Yugoslavia, for example, ethnic cleansing was carried out by the Croats as well as by the Serbs. So, before troops are committed, it is important to make clear where the guilt lies, who should be attacked, and who defended.

Genocide and National Interest

Some countries actively oppose intervention when it is in their national interests to do so—if, for example, they have a strong trading relationship with the government carrying out the genocide. In 1975, Indonesia invaded East Timor and perpetrated a genocide that resulted in the deaths of around 350,000 people. Western nations did not respond, and the genocide was ignored largely because Indonesia's oil reserves made it an important trading partner with the West.

The main stumbling block that defeats most attempts at international action against genocide is national interest. Countries are often unwilling to take action in a situation where their national interest isn't directly at risk. Preventing a genocide in a distant region with which they have little commercial or strategic interest is often not high on their list of priorities.

What Can the United Nations Do?

The United Nations is intended to be an official forum where nations can discuss matters of international concern. Unfortunately, the UN is often unable to act effectively to counter genocide, mainly because member states cannot agree

A contingent of UN peacekeeping troops from Turkey assembles for a patrol in Tyr, Lebanon, during 2006.

on what action should be taken. Any UN intervention must first be approved by the United Nations Security Council. The five permanent members of the Security Council—China, France, Britain, Russia, and the United States—have the power to reject the decisions of the others, effectively paralyzing the UN.

For example, in 1998 Serb forces were carrying out massacres, mass rapes, and deportations in Kosovo, a region of Serbia that had declared independence. Russia, which has historic ties to Serbia, threatened to veto any UN military action. This forced NATO to intervene without UN Security Council approval, making its actions illegal under international law. Russia's attitude caused a delay and therefore further loss of life in Kosovo. This has led some to argue for an elimination of the veto, or a restriction of its use in genocidal situations.

On occasion, UN intervention has been effective. In 1999, the people of East Timor voted to end the Indonesian occupation, begun in 1975, and become independent. In response, Indonesian troops and their supporters went on a rampage, killing hundreds of East Timorese and causing more than 250,000 people to flee into neighboring West Timor. The United Nations quickly condemned Indonesia's actions, and an Australian-led peacekeeping force soon stabilized the country and began preparing it for independence. East Timor became an independent nation in May of 2002.

Do Trials Work?

In 1945 and 1946, Nazi perpetrators of the Holocaust were put on trial in Nuremberg, while Japanese military and political

The first session of the International Tribunal on War Crimes in the Former Yugoslavia opens in the Hague, Netherlands, in 1993. The tribunal's 11 judges are seated behind the far table.

leaders were put on trial in Tokyo for their war crimes, including atrocities like the Rape of Nanking. These were the first times that international courts were set up to prosecute individuals for crimes against humanity. However, although the United Nations passed a Genocide Convention in 1948 that made genocide illegal, no further international trials were held for almost 50 years. This was because the members of the UN were divided by the Cold War, and many governments refused to accept the legitimacy of an international court.

General Ratko Mladic, commander of the Bosnian Serb army during the 1990s, has been on trial for genocide and crimes against humanity since 2012.

In 1993, an International Criminal Tribunal (temporary court) was set up to try those responsible for the genocides in the former Yugoslavia. A similar court was set up the following year to deal with the genocide in Rwanda. The International Criminal Tribunal for Rwanda had conducted about 60 trials by the time its work was completed in 2015. In addition, thousands of cases of lesser offenses have been prosecuted in gacaca courts. These were established in 2001 by Rwandan law to relieve the burden on the national justice system. According to the Gacacas' proponents, the governing principle in all the cases is to bring together all of the protagonists at the actual location of the crime, including the survivors, witnesses, and alleged perpetrators. Prisoners who confess to their guilt are released to return to their village or city, where the local gacaca court pronounces its judgment.

In July 2002, a permanent International Criminal Court (ICC) was created. Its purpose was to investigate and bring to justice individuals who commit genocide, crimes against humanity, and war crimes when the justice systems of individual states cannot or will not prosecute those offenses. Through 2015, thirty-six people had been indicted by the ICC.

The establishment of the tribunals sent an important message. Leaders contemplating genocide know that systems are now in place to prosecute them. However, the progress of the tribunals has been slow and the trials have been costly and time-consuming. Slobodan Milosevic, the former president of Serbia, was brought to trial in 2001 for his part in the genocide in Kosovo, but his trial was not yet completed when he died of a heart attack in 2006.

Others have escaped prosecution to date. In 2010, Sudanese president Omar al-Bashir became the first person convicted by the International Criminal Court on on charges of genocide, due to his involvement of government forces in the campaign against the Fur people of Darfur. However, despite this indictment, al-Bashir has never been arrested. He continues to serve as president of Sudan, and to move freely about that country.

It is too early to say whether the trial process is effective, or whether it will act as a deterrent to future genocides. It is certainly important for genocide survivors to know that a system of justice exists. However, there is a danger that these trials may disrupt the natural healing processes of a community. Lengthy court cases will keep the painful memories of the genocide fresh in the minds of those involved. This may fuel a desire for revenge, instead of allowing people to get on with rebuilding their lives.

Can We Live Together in Peace?

What are the prospects of a world without genocide? The characteristics of hatred, fear, and ruthlessness that drive people to commit this crime show no signs of disappearing from human

Public memorials, such as the Jewish Holocaust Memorial in Berlin, serve as reminders of past atrocities, as well as warnings about the threat of future genocides.

nature. So, prevention may be the only cure. As well as introducing measures to stop current or *impending* genocides, as described in this chapter; governments and organizations must also look at ways of preventing genocides in the long term.

The key to this is education, especially in communities that have been damaged by genocide. Here, young people are most at risk of getting sucked into a cycle of violence. They need to learn that all people, whatever their background, deserve respect. The common humanity and shared values of different cultures should be emphasized, by encouraging friendships between members of different communities, for example. It is also important to raise public awareness about past genocides. Understanding the causes and effects of mass murder is one way of helping people to see its evil.

Some countries have managed to avoid potential genocide. In South Africa and Northern Ireland, for example, bitterly divided communities are learning to live in peace. It is not an easy path to follow when prejudices run so deep, but these examples at least offer hope that a future without genocide may be possible.

Text-Dependent Questions

1. What is one of the biggest challenges in trying to stop genocides?
2. What are three things an international peacekeeping force can do to try to prevent massacres from taking place?
3. What organization must approve any UN intervention in a genocide situation?

Research Project

Using the Internet or your school library, do some research on the definition of genocide, and answer the following question: "Should foreign governments intervene militarily if they suspect a genocide is taking place within a certain country?" Those who support this premise will note that the lives of innocent victims often depend on the prompt intervention of outside forces. Those who oppose this premise believe that foreign governments should not meddle in the internal affairs of other countries. Write a two-page report, using data you've found in your research to support your conclusion.

Genocide by Continent, since 1900

AFRICA

Location: German South-West Africa (present-day Namibia)
Years: 1904–1908
Casualties: 34,000 to 110,000 Herero and Namaqua people
Perpetrators: Imperial Germany

Location: Ethiopia
Years: 1945–1974
Casualties: 150,000 Oromo, Eritreans, Somalis
Perpetrators: government of Haile Selassie

Location: Sudan
Years: 1956–1972
Casualties: 400,000 civilians, mostly of the Dinka, Nuer, and
   Azande ethnic groups
Perpetrators: government and military of Sudan

⬅

German soldiers arrest Polish Jews in Warsaw, 1943.

Location: Burundi
Years: 1959–1962
Casualties: 200,000 Hutus
Perpetrators: Tutsi government and army

Location: Biafra region of Nigeria
Years: 1966–1970
Casualties: 1 million people of the Ibo ethnic group.
Perpetrators: Nigerian army

Location: Equatorial Guinea
Years: 1968-1979
Casualties: approximately 80,000 members of the Bubi ethnic minority
Perpetrators: Macias Nguema government and army

Location: Burundi
Years: 1972
Casualties: 250,000 Hutus
Perpetrators: Tutsi government and army

Location: Uganda
Years: 1972–1979
Casualties: 300,000 people of the Acholi, Lango, and Karamoja ethnic group
Perpetrators: Idi Amin government and Ugandan military

Location: Ethiopia
Years: 1974–1979
Casualties: 750,000 Oromo and others considered "enemies"
Perpetrators: Derg (communist) government

Location: Uganda
Years: 1980–1986
Casualties: 250,000 Baganda, Banyarwanda people
Perpetrators: regime of Milton Obote

Location: Sudan
Years: 1983–2002
Casualties: more than 2 million Dinka, Nuer, and Azande
Perpetrators: government and military of Sudan

Location: Burundi
Years: 1993
Casualties: 50,000 Tutsis, 100,000 Hutus
Perpetrators: Tutsis and Hutus

Location: Liberia
Years: 1990–2002
Casualties: 100,000 Krahn, Gio, and Mano ethnic peoples
Perpetrators: Liberian government and army

Location: Democratic Republic of the Congo
Years: 1994–2002
Casualties: 170,000 Hutus, Banyamulenge, Heme, Lendu
Perpetrators: Ugandan, Rwandan, and Congolese armies

Location: Rwanda
Years: 1994
Casualties: about 800,000 Tutsis and moderate Hutus.
Perpetrators: Hutus government and people

Location: Darfur region of western Sudan
Years: 2003–2010
Casualties: about 400,000 Africans of the Fur, Zaghawa, and Masalit ethnic groups
Perpetrators: Janjaweed ethnic Arab militias, supported by the Sudanese government of Omar al-Bashir.

EUROPE and the MIDDLE EAST

Location: Ottoman Empire (present-day Turkey, Armenia, and neighboring areas)
Years: 1915–1923
Casualties: 1.5 million Armenians, roughly 1 million Assyrians, Greeks, Kurds, and others
Perpetrators: military of the Ottoman Empire

Location: Ukraine region of the Soviet Union
Years: 1932–1933
Casualties: about 7 million
Perpetrators: Famine (*Holodomor*) intentionally caused by Soviet government policies of Joseph Stalin in order to eliminate Ukranian nationalists.

Location: German-occupied Europe

Years: 1933–1945

Casualties: At least 6 million Jews, as well as 500,000 Gypsies (Romani) and others designated as undesirable by the Nazi government.

Perpetrators: Nazi Germany led by Adolf Hitler

Location: Soviet Union

Years: 1945–1991

Casualties: 15 million "class enemies," including members of the Karachai, Crimean Tatar, and Balkar ethnic groups and religious minorities

Perpetrators: Soviet government, army, and secret police

Location: Poland

Years: 1945–1981

Casualties: 1.5 million ethnic Germans

Perpetrators: Soviet government

Location: Iran

Years: 1953–1978

Casualties: 260,000 government enemies

Perpetrators: SAVAK (the Shah's secret police)

Location: Lebanon

Years: 1974–1991

Casualties: 55,000 Christians, Muslims, and Druze

Perpetrators: religious militias

Location: Iran
Years: 1978–1992
Casualties: 60,000 Kurds, monarchists, Bahai
Perpetrators: Iranian government of Ayatollah Khomeini

Location: Iraq
Years: 1986–1989
Casualties: 200,000 Kurds
Perpetrators: The military of Iraq, led by Saddam Hussein, which used chemical weapons and other means to eliminate the Kurds as part of the Anfal Campaign.

Location: Bosnia, Croatia
Years: 1992–1998
Casualties: 250,000 Muslims, Croats, and Serbs
Perpetrators: Bosnian Serbs, Croats

Location: Bosnia
Years: 1995
Casualties: 8,500 Muslims
Perpetrators: Serbian military, commanded by General Ratko Mladiç, during the Bosnian War (1992–1995)

NORTH AND SOUTH AMERICA

Location: Brazil
Years: 1945–1964
Casualties: 300,000 indigenous people
Perpetrators: Brazilian government and settler militias

Location: Guatemala
Years: 1950s–1980s
Casualties: 200,000 Mayans
Perpetrators: Guatemalan government and army

ASIA

Location: China
Years: 1937–1938
Casualties: approximately 300,000 Chinese civilians and disarmed troops in Nanking
Perpetrators: Imperial Japanese Army

Location: People's Republic of China
Years: 1949–present
Casualties: over 35 million "class enemies" and religious minorities
Perpetrators: Chinese communist government, army, and police

Location: North Vietnam
Years: 1954–1975
Casualties: 1.7 million class enemies and ethnic minorities
Perpetrators: North Vietnamese government

Location: Tibet
Years: 1959–1990s
Casualties: 1.6 million Tibetan Buddhists
Perpetrators: Chinese government

Location: Burma (Myanmar)
Years: 1962–78
Casualties: 100,000 Shan, Muslims, Karen, Christians
Perpetrators: Burmese government

Location: Indonesia
Years: 1965–1966
Casualties: 500,000 communists
Perpetrators: Indonesian military and militias supported by Suharto

Location: East Pakistan (present-day Bangladesh)
Years: 1971
Casualties: 1.5 million Hindus and Bengalis
Perpetrators: Pakistani Army

Location: Cambodia
Years: 1975–1979
Casualties: between 1.7 million and 3 million people, especially Cham Muslims, city people, and ethnic Vietnamese
Perpetrators: Khmer Rouge regime led by Pol Pot

Location: East Timor
Years: 1975–2000
Casualties: 350,000 East Timorese
Perpetrators: Indonesian army, militias

Location: North Korea

Years: 1994-present

Casualties: estimated 2 to 3 million dissidents and ethnic
minorities

Perpetrators: communist government and military

Location: Afghanistan

Years: 1996–2001

Casualties: 50,000 + Tajiks, Uzbeks, and Hazara people

Perpetrators: Taliban government

Location: Sri Lanka

Years: 2009

Casualties: more than 40,000 civilians of the Tamil ethnic
group

Perpetrators: Sri Lankan military and government

International Organizations

United Nations High Commissioner for Human Rights
Administrative Section
Office of the United Nations
High Commissioner for Human Rights
Palais des Nations
CH-1211 Geneva 10, Switzerland
Phone: + 41 22 917 90 20
E-mail: InfoDesk@ohchr.org
Website: www.ohchr.org/english

Amnesty International
5 Penn Plaza
14th Floor
New York, NY 10001
Phone: (212) 807-8400
E-mail: aimember@aiusa.org
Website: www.amnestyusa.org

Human Rights Watch
350 Fifth Ave.
34th Floor
New York, NY 10118-3299
Phone: (212) 290-4700
E-mail: hrwnyc@hrw.org
Website: www.hrw.org

International Crisis Group

149 Avenue Louise Level 24 B-1050
Brussels, Belgium
Phone: + 32-2-502 90 38
Fax: + 32-2-502 50 38
Email: brussels@crisisgroup.org
Website: www.crisisgroup.org

International Alert

346 Clapham Road
London SW9 9AP United Kingdom
Phone: + 44 (0) 20 7627 6800
Fax: + 44 (0) 20 7627 6900
Website: www.international-alert.org

International Criminal Court

Maanweg, 174 2516 AB
The Hague The Netherlands
Phone: + 31 (0)70 515 8515
Fax: + 31 (0)70 515 8555
Email: otp.informationdesk@icc-cpi.int
Website: www.icc-cpi.int/home.html

Coalition Against Genocide

8480 Baltimore National Pike, #286
Ellicott City, MD 21043
Phone: (443) 927 9039
Fax: (443) 927 9039
Email: info@coalitionagainstgenocide.org
Website: www.coalitionagainstgenocide.org

Series Glossary

apartheid—literally meaning "apartness," the political policies of the South African government from 1948 until the early 1990s designed to keep peoples segregated based on their color.

BCE and CE—alternatives to the traditional Western designation of calendar eras, which used the birth of Jesus as a dividing line. BCE stands for "Before the Common Era," and is equivalent to BC ("Before Christ"). Dates labeled CE, or "Common Era," are equivalent to *Anno Domini* (AD, or "the Year of Our Lord").

colony—a country or region ruled by another country.

democracy—a country in which the people can vote to choose those who govern them.

detention center—a place where people claiming asylum and refugee status are held while their case is investigated.

ethnic cleansing—an attempt to rid a country or region of a particular ethnic group. The term was first used to describe the attempt by Serb nationalists to rid Bosnia of Muslims.

house arrest—to be detained in your own home, rather than in prison, under the constant watch of police or other government forces, such as the army.

reformist—a person who wants to improve a country or an institution, such as the police force, by ridding it of abuses or faults.

republic—a country without a king or queen, such as the US.

United Nations—an international organization set up after the end of World War II to promote peace and co-operation throughout the world. Its predecessor was the League of Nations.

UN Security Council—the permanent committee of the United Nations that oversees its peacekeeping operations around the world.

World Bank—an international financial organization, connected to the United Nations. It is the largest source of financial aid to developing countries.

World War I—A war fought in Europe from 1914 to 1918, in which an alliance of nations that included Great Britain, France, Russia, Italy, and the United States defeated the alliance of Germany, Austria-Hungary, the Ottoman Empire, and Bulgaria.

World War II—A war fought in Europe, Africa, and Asia from 1939 to 1945, in which the Allied Powers (the United States, Great Britain, France, the Soviet Union, and China) worked together to defeat the Axis Powers (Germany, Italy, and Japan).

Further Reading

Bloxham, Donald, and A. Dirk Moses. *The Oxford Handbook of Genocide Studies*. New York: Oxford University Press, 2013.

Cockett, Richard. *Sudan: Darfur and the Failure of an African State*. New Haven: Yale University Press, 2010.

Jones, Adam. *Genocide: A Comprehensive Introduction*. 2nd ed. New York: Routledge, 2011.

Koopmans, Andy. *Rwanda*. Philadelphia: Mason Crest, 2012.

Power, Samantha. *"A Problem from Hell": America and the Age of Genocide*. New York: Basic Books, 2013.

Pritchard, Maria. *Genocide: A History from Carthage to Darfur*. London: RW Press, 2013.

Snyder, Timothy. *Black Earth: The Holocaust as History and Warning*. New York: Tim Duggan Books, 2015.

Walzer, Michael. *Just and Unjust Wars: A Moral Argument with Historical Illustrations*. New York: Basic Books, 2015.

Internet Resources

http://www.un.org/en/preventgenocide/adviser
> Official website of the United Nations Special Adviser on the Prevention of Genocide, who acts as a catalyst to raise awareness of the causes and dynamics of genocide, and to advocate and mobilize for appropriate action as needed.

https://www.amnesty.org/en
> The website of Amnesty International, a group that works to protect human rights worldwide.

http://www.ushmm.org/wlc/en/article.php?ModuleId = 10
007095
> This timeline noting the major conceptual and legal advances in the development of "genocide" is provided by the United States Holocaust Memorial Museum.

http://endgenocide.org
> United to End Genocide is an international organization that fights to protect all who face the threat of genocide or mass atrocity, anywhere in the world.

http://genocidewatch.net
> Genocide Watch exists to predict, prevent, stop, and punish genocide and other forms of mass murder. This non-governmental organization is attempting to build an international movement to prevent and stop genocide.

http://www.savedarfur.org

The Save Darfur Coalition was formed to raise awareness about the crisis in Darfur.

http://www.inogs.com/

The International Network of Genocide Scholars (INoGS) was founded 2005 in Berlin. This nonprofit organization fosters scholarly exchange and academic debate on all aspects of genocide.

http://www.genocideeducation.org

The Genocide Education Project is a nonprofit organization that assists educators in teaching about human rights and genocide.

Index

Numbers in **bold italics** refer to captions.

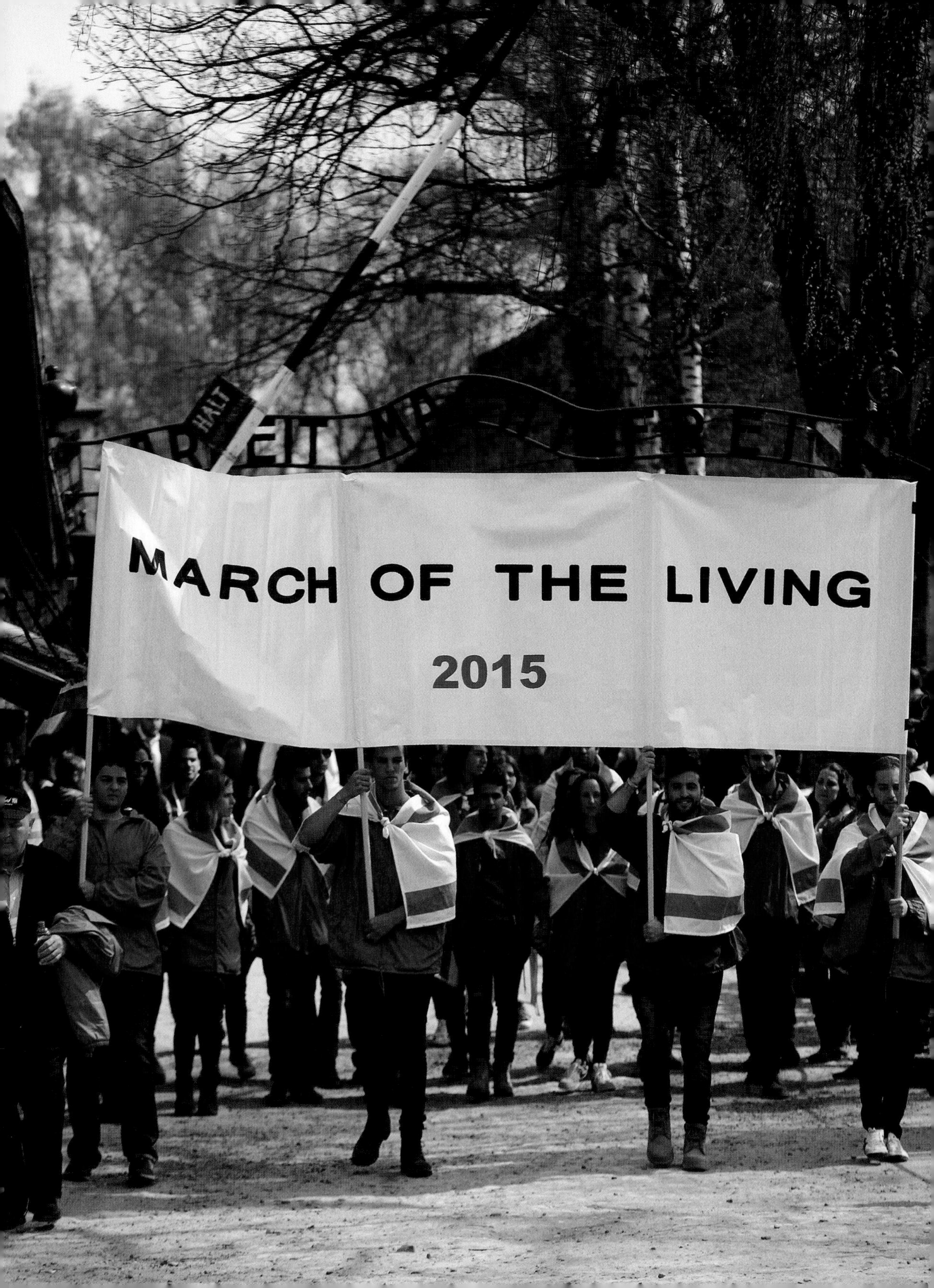
HALT
MARCH OF THE LIVING
2015

About the Author

Albert Ward is a freelance writer who specializes in history and politics. He has written books on subjects ranging from the Wall Street Crash to terrorism.